EXPLORING SMALL TOWNS
2. NORTHERN CALIFORNIA

exploring
SMALL TOWNS

2. NORTHERN CALIFORNIA

david yeadon
the ward ritchie press

FOR LYNNE

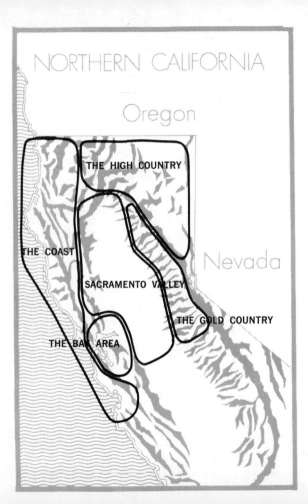

Contents

Introduction

There was a day when I almost gave up. I was sitting alone in my camper in a mist shrouded forest way up north of Shasta and feeling very sorry for myself. The gas in the stove had run out and the half cooked steak in the pan sat in a pool of hard fat: the heater refused to work and a bucket-full of torrential rain from outside had leaked through the windows, across my manuscript, onto the floor, and felt to be slowly turning into ice.

In an unusually romantic frame of mind I began thinking of the settlers who had slowly dragged their way across the plains, deserts, and mountains into California many decades ago. I thought of their struggles through the untraversed rock-blocked canyons of the deserts, their dismay at early winters which filled the Sierra passes with snow and barred their only way through to California and their great gasps of wonderment and relief as they finally entered the great central valley. I remembered too, the legendary pioneers: Gaspar de Portola, Junipero Serra, Jedediah Smith, Peter Lassen, John Fremont, Kit Carson, and John Sutter, whose stubborn wills and enthusiasm had smashed down the barriers of fear and despair and set their stamp on one of the greatest States in the Union.

I thought of all this; then I dried my manuscript and continued writing.

Even though I have travelled for tens of thousands of miles throughout California I never cease to marvel at the tangibility of the State's history. The important events which shaped the State's development and which are now recorded in countless historical tomes, occured mostly, little over a century ago. The wheel scratches of pioneer waggons can still be found in the deep Sierra canyons. Only recently a locket belonging to one of the original members of the Donner Party was discovered on the old Donner trail near Lake Tahoe. Way out across the searing expanses of the high desert, it is still possible to come across the undisturbed grave of some dream-filled pioneer who never quite made it to the illusionary nirvana which was to become California.

As I explored some of the small and lesser known towns of the State, I was constantly exhilarated by this sense of history-come-alive. Fortunately it would appear that my sense of awe is shared by many. I found, in northern California particularly, a real concern for the constructive retention of California's heritage. Whether as a result of subdued development pressures or a greater educated awareness of the population, there appears to be a real recognition of the need to safeguard and treasure important landmarks which reflect the stages of California's growth. There is an appreciation of the value of historical perspective expressed physically in the form of buildings and "places."

Nevertheless, there are problems. State organizations have little capital available for this kind of investment and local historical societies are often even more constrained by financial limitations. To date there has still been too little active concern given to the selective retention of significant facets of California's development. Hopefully, this small book may provoke an increased concern and stimulate a dedicated effort to keep and guard what is left of a very fragile but important heritage.

ACKNOWLEDGMENTS

There are countless scores of people without whose encouragement and assistance I would have found it impossible to complete this book—librarians who gave generously of their time to assist my research; residents in the communities I visited who gave me new insights into the richness of California's history; and fellow-travellers who led me to many towns I might otherwise have missed.

First and foremost, however, is my wife Anne who accompanied me on all my travels and withstood the tempests of my worst moods. Without her work, patience, understanding and love, this book would be no more than a dog-eared manuscript in some dresser-drawer.

Then there are our friends who provided for all our needs from mailing service and martinis to bed, breakfast and benevolence. To Bob and Holly and Rachel, Moe and Marcia, Fereydoon, Elizabeth, Garth, Sally, Buff, Peggy, Barbara, Fred and Cheree (not forgetting Clara) we extend our sincerest gratitude.

ABOUT THE AUTHOR

David Yeadon is a city planner who tired of big-city life in Los Angeles and set out to explore those hidden parts of California, which too few of us have a chance to see.

Mr. Yeadon, who has spent much of his life in Europe and the Middle East, is fascinated by the tangible and short history of California. During his months of travel through back lanes and tiny villages, he spent much of his time talking to local inhabitants and pouring over time-worn books in dusty libraries in an effort to capsulize the fascinating history of the small, often little-known towns scattered around the northern half of the State.

Small Towns is the result and Mr. Yeadon hopes that his sketches and notes will generate a fresh interest in those parts of California still largely undiscovered by tourists and residents alike.

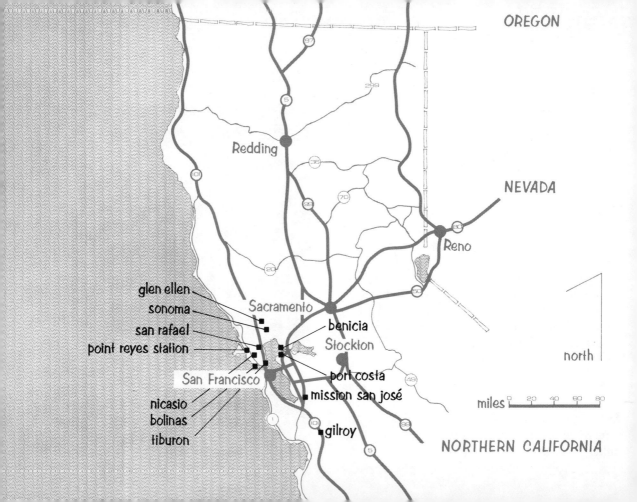

The Bay Area

The beauties of San Francisco and its hinterland have long provided songwriters, poets and painters with an almost inexhaustible supply of inspiration. Its fascination stems partly from its ludicrous location on some of the steepest hills of any city in the world; partly from the richness of its architecture and its cultural background and partly from the unique juxtaposition of wild mountain scenery and dense urban development.

The nature of the topography and the idiosyncracies of San Francisco's growth are such that within a few miles of downtown, tiny unspoiled communities exist which appear to have changed little since the turn of the century. Bolinas, Nicasio, Point Reyes Station and Mission San José all retain their distinct characters and although they are slowly becoming commuter or retirement centers in disguise, at least they have chosen not to flaunt the fact over the landscape.

The small communities immediately adjacent to the Bay and the Sacramento River reflect the various stages of San Francisco's growth. Benicia and Port Costa were both once flourishing communities, the former as a one-time State capital and major supply center at the time of the gold rush, the latter as hub of the great grain warehouses which once lined the rocky southern shore of the Sacramento and provided a much needed outlet for wheat from the delta and valley. Both towns succumbed to the overwhelming dynamism of San Francisco and today are merely remnants of a former glory.

A third town, Tiburon, accommodated some of the first "overspill" from the city—families searching for clean air on the northern bay-shore. Its fortunes still seem to be steadily increasing as the town acts as an important recreational center, second only to Sausalito.

Benicia

CAPITAL FOR A YEAR

General Vallejo had a passion for establishing towns and this one, originally named Santa Francisca after his wife, was one of his favorites. He had great plans for its development as a major Bayside city but as the Gold Rush fever grew in the 1850's it became clear that Yerba Buena (renamed San Francisco) was becoming a potential threat to his aspirations. Vallejo, not to be outdone, rechristened his town Benicia and set out to promote its growth as a waypoint serving traffic to the gold country. For a while his plans succeeded and in 1853 Benicia's prosperity earned it the title of state capital—which it promptly lost again in 1854!

The town went through subsequent phases as a military headquarters, coaling and repair center for river boats and a food canning center. But somehow it could never regain its fleeting glory. San Francisco dominated as the major commerce and trading center in the Bay area and Benicia became a docile, orderly town, proud of its monuments.

BENICIA CAPITOL

Bolinas OLD BARN · BOLINAS

THE SAD STORY OF CAPTAIN EASKOOT
The quiet, almost hidden community of Bolinas has more than its fair share of legendary

folk figures. One of the most distinguished is Captain Easkoot—or rather, the ghost of Captain Easkoot. He lived in the huge white mansion which overlooks the Bay. Following the premature death of his wife and a traumatic incident in which her coffin was washed out to sea by an unusually high flood tide as it was being taken to the cemetery, the Captain became an embittered man. His ire was increased by the fact that his hook-hand (all notorious captains seem to have one!) disappeared during the funeral wake. He spent the rest of his life chasing innocent travellers away from the bay which he considered to be his property and, even now on stormy nights, his ghost haunts the town looking for the lost hand.

During the 1850's Bolinas was a major logging center for San Francisco. Although over 15 million feet of lumber was felled in the area, the town's prosperity dwindled with the demise of the gold rush. Subsequent periods of potato farming, coal, copper, oil and asbestos mining, shipbuilding and even rum-running and opium smuggling were all shortlived. The bay became silted and Bolinas never grew.

BOLINAS MAIN STREET

Gilroy   FRUIT STAND NEAR GILROY

A POOR SCOTSMAN AND A
WEALTHY GERMAN

Gilroy's founder citizen was a hearty Scotsman named John Cameron who fled from Monterey in 1814 after delivering a "knuckle sandwich" to a British naval officer. He settled in the

Santa Clara valley, changed his name to Gilroy and became a ranch-owner after marrying into a Mexican family. Although he had a reputation for generosity, Gilroy eventually gambled himself into "absolute want" and lived off charity from the "British Benevolent Society"!

John Gilroy's fluctuating fortunes contrasted sharply with the empire-building fame of Henry Miller, a German butcher, who made his headquarters just south of Gilroy and built up a million acre ranch holding throughout California (Miller often boasted that he could ride horseback from Mexico to Canada and spend each night at one of his own ranches!).

Gilroy's Italianate/Mongolian styled town hall is the town's most prominent building. Unfortunately, due to the fact that this magnificent edifice is considered to be earthquake-prone, it is currently unused. However, the local historical society hopes to raise sufficient funds for restoration & possible usage as a museum.

Folksy fruit stands, crammed with ripe fruits and smothered in hand-painted signs, are a common sight north of Gilroy along 101. This one is particularly notable.

JACK LONDON'S WOLF HOUSE

Glen Ellen

HOME OF JACK LONDON

Jack London is one of the twentieth century's most renowned author-adventurers. In the course of his short life (1876-1916), he wrote over fifty books (including "White Fang" and "The Call of The Wild") in addition to travelling the south seas in his boat "The Snark," panning for gold in the Klondike, leading fur-trapping expeditions in the Yukon and acting as journalist-correspondent during the Boer and Russo-Japanese wars.

The ruins of his Wolf House can be visited at the Jack London State Historic Park in the Sonoma Valley just above the tiny community of Glen Ellen (Glen Ellen seems particularly proud of Jack's reputation as a drinker—the local bars all claim to have been "Jack's favorite"!). This was to have been a 26-room mansion complete with internal courtyard. Its walls, more than 18" thick were built of huge volcanic boulders dragged by horses from a nearby quarry. Unfortunately, a few days before the Londons were due to move in, this magnificent structure was completely gutted by fire. The house was never rebuilt and Jack died a little while later at the age of forty.

MAIN STREET · GLEN ELLEN

MISSION SAN JOSE
DE GUADALUPE

Mission San Jose

JEDEDIAH SMITH'S JAIL

What appears to be the main building is only a partial remnant of the once elaborate Mission del Gloriosisimo Patriarcha Señor San Jose de Guadalupe. The delicately spired church stands on the foundation of the original Mission Church which was totally leveled during an earthquake in October, 1868.

The Mission was founded in 1797 and developed as a strategic point for inland explorations. Jedediah Smith, one of California's earliest traveller/explorers visited here in 1827 during one of his many wide-ranging expeditions, only to find himself jailed by a wary priest. Eventually, he was released by order of the governor and allowed to use the Mission as a refurbishing center. According to his journal, he was particularly impressed by the musical accompaniment during Mission services which "consisted of twelve or fifteen violins, five base vials and one flute."

Although close to the Bay Area conurbation, the little community of Mission San Jose has managed to preserve its distinct character.

Nicasio

THE LITTLE GIRL OF NICASIO

Somewhere in this tiny community there lies the body of a little girl. She was one of the daughters of the Carey family who moved into the area in 1852. The family tried hard to make a living off the land but after a few years decided to try their luck elsewhere. Before they had a chance to leave, however, their young daughter died and was buried by the side of a large oak tree near the village square. A long time later, the Careys returned wishing to give the body a proper burial. Unfortunately, the village had changed—the oak tree had been felled and a large hotel had been erected on the site of their old homestead. They never found their daughter and to this day, she lies somewhere near the square. Some say that on quiet evenings, she can be heard weeping very softly.

Nicasio's little white church is a well-known painters' subject. The original church was erected in the mid 1880's and underwent a major reconstruction in 1905. It still remains, however, one of the most perfect New England influenced churches in Northern California.

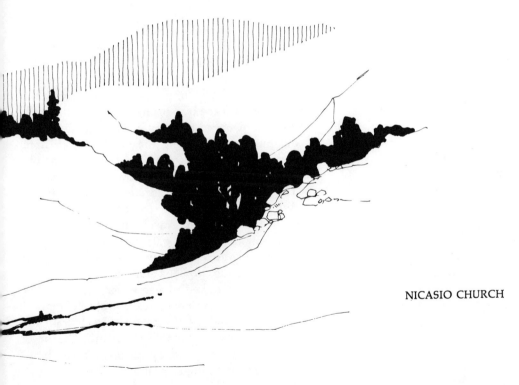

NICASIO CHURCH

Port Costa

POST OFFICE • PORT COSTA

BILL RICH'S TOWN

In 1965 Port Costa was a condemned town, destined to die a slow lingering death alongside the Sacramento River. Today it is a fascinating community of antique shops and fine restaurants —the brain child of ex-beer truck driver, Bill Rich. Bill, backed by a team of enthusiastic workers, has managed to renovate most of the town's old buildings including the old Victorian hotel and the Bull Valley Inn—a bold brownstone structure built by a skilled Swiss stone mason. The huge Warehouse, located across from the Bull Inn was erected in 1878 from volcanic rock carried as ballast in Australian merchant ships. The building formed part of a whole string of long warehouses which lined the rocky coast near Port Costa and provided shipping centers for the grain grown in the Delta and Sacramento Valley.

Bill is still working enthusiastically to improve his "town" and his "Warehouse" restaurant has attracted much favorable comment. The decor can only be described as "inspired bric-a-brac" and it is truly a unique creation.

MAIN STREET • PORT COSTA

THE SAND CASTLE • POINT REYES STATION

Point Reyes Station

HAUNT OF MOUNTAIN BEAVERS AND TUFTED PUFFINS

A few miles west of the small agrarian community of Point Reyes Station is Drakes Bay and the Point Reyes Peninsula, a bleak stretch of coastline known for its notorious fogs. Controversy still rages as to whether that buccaneer-courtier Sir Francis Drake actually landed here or some other point on the coast. His log reference to a "fair and good bay" hardly coincides with the subsequent reputation of Point Reyes as a graveyard for ships. Ever since 1855 when an English clipper was dashed to pieces on the rocks here, the Point has claimed a long string of victims and even after 1870 when a lighthouse was erected, disasters continued to occur at regular intervals. If this indeed is the "fair and good bay" of Drake's records, he must have arrived at a particularly fortuituous time!

The Peninsula itself is a wild stretch of moorland, once the home of the now-vanished Roosevelt Elk and still populated by the rare mountain beaver and tufted puffins. It's fine walking country. On the inland side the strange sunken valley of Tomales Bay (dramatic evidence of the San Andreas earthquake fault) provides a secluded haven for a wealth of birdlife.

Point Reyes Station sits at the southern end of the Bay. Nearby Olema used to be the main town in the area and in the early 1800's did a steady trade with the Russian fur-trappers based at Fort Ross. At that time Tomales Bay stretched as far south as Olema and enabled transportation of grain and cattle by "lighter."

However, subsequent shrinking of the Bay coupled with the selection of Point Reyes Station as a railroad stop on the narrow gauge railroad to Bodega, led to Olema's decline.

Point Reyes Station today is a quiet community. The railroad has long been closed down but the sheds still stand across from the "Sandcastle" —a fine building, originally a Foresters lodge, which was recently converted into an interesting home and art gallery by Bill and Jean Booras.

ST. VINCENTS SCHOOL

San Rafael

THE ST. VINCENTS SCHOOL FOR BOYS

If you look closely as you drive along the 101 just north of San Rafael, you'll notice an elaborate towered structure set well back from the road, down a long avenue of trees. This is part of the St. Vincents School for Boys which was originally established in 1855 by the Sisters of Charity on land deeded to the organization by Timothy Murphy, an Irish-born immigrant. Mr. Murphy was well-regarded by the Mexicans after his arrival in California in 1828. General Vallejo in particular was impressed by his "commanding presence" and in addition to granting him land offered his daughter in marriage. Although the marriage never materialized, Timothy Murphy, who was renamed Don Timoteo Murphy, remained in good favor with the Mexicans and acted as civil administrator of the San Rafael Mission until 1842.

The school provides a home for boys of broken families. Although it appears to be a major historical monument, the main church, surrounded by terraced gardens, courtyards, and statues, is a mere fifty years old.

Sonoma

HOME OF THE BEAR FLAG REPUBLIC

The gentle Sonoma valley, rechristened "The Valley of the Moon" by novelist Jack London, provided the setting for many of the crucial episodes of California history during the 1830's and 40's. It was in Sonoma in June 1846 that California was declared an independent republic and the famous Bear Flag (made by William Todd —a nephew of Mrs. Abraham Lincoln) was raised on a flagpole in the main square. The republic was shortlived; in July the American Navy captured Monterey and claimed California for the U.S.A. No blood was spilt, no executions occurred—in fact everyone seemed to be relatively content with the situation. Even the Mexican General, Mariano Guadalupe Vallejo, who had been sent to Sonoma in 1834 to guard against the regular "takeover" threats by Russian, English and French entrepreneurs, was not displeased with the turn of events. Shortly afterward, he became a vintner of note; he also served twice as Sonoma's mayor and became the area's first state senator.

33

CHRISTIAN BROTHERS
NOVITIATE

Sonoma's Mission, San Francisco Solano was founded by Father Jose Altimira in 1823 and was the last of the missions built in California—the only one established under Mexican rule.

The Sonoma valley's current fame as one of California's quality wine producing regions dates back to Vallejo's period when he and the Hungarian vintner, Agoston Harazthy, competed to produce the finest possible wines. Harazthy, often called "The Father of California Viticulture" imported hundreds of root stocks at his own expense from Europe which he gave away gladly to other enthusiastic vintners in the area. Ironically, cuttings from these original stocks were exported back to Europe during the 1870's to replenish the thousands of acres of French, German and Italian vines destroyed by the phylloxera disease (loyal Californians are not slow to remind European wine snobs of this fact).

A little way to the east of Sonoma at Mount Lesalle is one of the most attractive of all California wineries—The Christian Brothers Cellars and Novitiate. In common with many others in the wine valley, the cellars are open for tours and tasting on a regular basis.

HOP BARN NEAR HEALDSBURG

An unusual anomaly in the prosperous wine country is this old hop barn which is kept in immaculate condition as a reminder of the past beer-brewing associations of the area.

Tiburon

A BUDDING SAUSALITO

This charming bay town is slowly becoming a second Sausalito complete with trinket shops and high quality restaurants. Fortunately the tourist trade is still of relatively modest proportions and the town, to date, has managed to avoid the disastrous traffic muddles which are the weekend plague of Sausalito.

Tiburon, named after the small sharks (tiburon) found in this part of the bay, became a significant community in 1884 when the rail service from San Rafael to Point Tiburon was joined by a ferry linking the area to San Francisco. Around this time Dr. Benjamin Lyford announced the development of his famous "Lyfords Hygeia" subdivision which today is marked by a stone tower on the northern fringe of town. It was expressly designed for those wishing to escape the "foul air" of San Francisco—apparently smog is not a twentieth century product!

The Tiburon Vintners' (part of Windsor Winery) tasting room is one of the town's most notable buildings and was once a fine boarding house (some locals claim a more accurate description would be "bawdy" house!).

TIBURON VINTNERS

The High Country

To many, the northeastern sector of California is an alien land, a bleak, often tundra-like landscape punctuated by brittle mountain ranges and wild, unwooded areas of lava plateaux.

To the initiated, the high country contains a romance and excitement unsurpassed in most other parts of the State. It was in this desolate region that thousands of travel-worn settlers caught their first glimpse of the almost mythical land of California. Observant walkers can still find signs of old campsites and trails used by the original settlers as they crossed the Walker Range and the Sierras before finally arriving at Sutters Fort in the Sacramento Valley. The small communities in the region such as Cedarville, Lake City, Fort Bidwell and Janesville have changed little since the 1860's when the first pioneer-farmers left the westward-bound wagon trains and set up home in Surprise Valley and around Honey Lake.

Their early days were not without troubles. This was Indian country and two of the most powerful and civilized tribes in northern California, the Modocs and Paiutes, regarded this land as their own and resented any attempts by "pale-faces" to settle permanently. The Modocs were particularly outraged by any invasion of their territory and waged an almost continuous war on the early settlers. It was not until the Modoc War of 1872-73, one of the most costly Indian campaigns in American history, that the U.S. Cavalry finally destroyed the Modoc threat. This was a furious battle which lasted for almost six months and centered around "Captain Jack's stronghold" in what is today the Lava Beds National Monument. Most of the tribe was wiped out and "Captain Jack," the Modoc chief, was hanged at Fort Klamath in October 1873.

The western sector of the high country fringes on the Sierras. This was an important gold mining and lumbering area. Although most of the early "placer" communities have long since vanished, Johnsville remains as a silent reminder of this frantic era of California history. McCloud and Westwood, both lumber communities, are still flourishing towns with some fine specimens of the early wood architecture.

The Cedarville Area

A LITTLE-KNOWN PART OF THE OLD WEST

East of Alturas over the steep Warner Range is a long narrow basin, appropriately named Surprise Valley by weary emigrants who, having travelled for weeks across the blistering Nevada desert on their journey westward, suddenly descended into this quiet pastoral enclave which abounded with rich vegetation and wildlife.

Today the area is little changed. Warm winds ripple the lakes which cover most of the valley floor; eagles circle the tall peaks of the Warner Range; mule deer, racoons, porcupines and skunks abound in the brush on the valley slopes.

Cedarville is the main community in the valley and was the location of the Cressler and Bonner Trading Post which provided much needed supplies for the emigrants preparing to cross over the Warners on their way to the Pacific. The main street still has all the characteristics of an old western town.

41

A little further up the valley is the tiny community of Lake City which once boasted a flourishing flour mill, a cheese processing plant, stores, and a two story hotel. Today the town is in a state of romantic decay.

Fort Bidwell, the northernmost community, is famous for its clusters of tall lombardy poplars, an unusually cultured feature in such a natural setting. The Fort, which today is largely in ruins, was established in 1866 as an army outpost to protect early settlers from attacks by the Paiute Indians. Fortunately these attacks were rare, although records show that a man named Townsend who originally founded the trading store in Cedarville, met an unpleasant end at the hands of local Indians in 1867.

By 1892 Indian problems had ceased in the area and the fort was turned over to the Department of Interior for use as an Indian school. Activities continued here until 1930 when the fort was abandoned to subsequent decay. The huge old barns in the area, many of which are in ruins, tell of a more prosperous era in the valley.

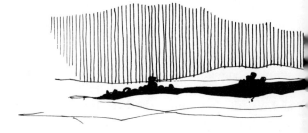

OLD BARN • FT. BIDWELL

JANESVILLE MOTEL

Janesville

THE ART OF CLYDE KNOX

Clyde Knox, a retired plasterer, sat outside his wooden shack in a rough armchair carved from a solid tree trunk and talked of the days when Janesville was a prosperous agricultural town in the heart of Indian country. Its original settlers, known locally as the "never sweats" because of the ease of working the rich farming land around Honey Lake, built a log fort to ward off bands of hostile Indians. However, the "fort" was rarely used and later became an elementary school.

A few years ago the town was bypassed, much to the annoyance of Clyde Knox who had spent many long months constructing his teepee-styled motel, complete with totempoles built mainly out of license plates. Today, however, he is philosophical about his fate. He enjoys the peace of the area and an occasional chat with tourists who stop to wander around his strange creation.

Janesville was once part of "Nataqua," a huge undefined area, which encompassed most of Modoc County and a large portion of present-day Nevada. This illegal empire was the creation of Isaac Roop, one of the first settlers in the Honey Lake area. He and a band of local settlers met in the Roop cabin (still preserved in Susanville) on April 26, 1856 and founded the territory; Roop was appointed Secretary of this unusual little governing body and Peter Lassen, whose fame (and later notoriety) as an expedition leader was well known in the area, was made surveyor. Nataqua however was short-lived and exists today only in the minds of some of the older residents.

Johnsville

THE FIRST SKI CLUB IN THE WEST

The Mother Lode Gold Rush of 1849 quickly spread over onto the east side of the Sierras. As was usually the case, the first settlements were "tent-cities" inhabited by transient hardy "placer" miners who spent long cold days dredging the silt from stream beds in pursuit of elusive bonanzas.

Placer mining was later overshadowed by hard-rock mining. Large companies, backed by ample funds from American and European investers, dug, blasted and burrowed into the mountains following irregular gold veins embedded deep in quartz strata. Johnsville was the company town for a London-based consortium, the Sierra Buttes Mining Co. Ltd., which for twenty years, until the early 90's, enjoyed huge profits from its Eureka Peak Mine. The town's other claim to fame was its ski club—the first in the Western hemisphere.

46

MAIN STREET

JOHNSVILLE

L&C LIVERY

McCLOUD HOTEL

McCloud

A TRUE LUMBER TOWN

This small neat community sits in wooded foothills under the shadow of California's Kilamanjaro—Mount Shasta. The town preserves, under the guise of phonetic spelling, the name of the Scot, Alexander Roderick McLeod, who in 1827 led the first band of Hudson's Bay company trappers into northern California.

The great McCloud Hotel, built in 1918 to replace an earlier structure destroyed by fire, and the adjoining barn-like building which was once a huge dining hall, tell of the days when the town was first founded as the headquarters of the Mc-Cloud Lumber Co. There were once many similar over-sized structures which were built as rooming houses for the company's lumberjacks. Note the steep roofs of the hotel which suggest heavy snowfalls during the winter months.

The logging railroad known as the McCloud River Railroad linked the Southern Pacific at Mount Shasta with the Great Northern in Big

OLD CHURCH · McCLOUD

Valley. It still operates as a freight carrier and during the summer months special passenger coaches are added for tourists who take day-long excursions into the dense forests around the slopes of Mount Shasta.

In 1954 the town received a boost when the McCloud Lumber Company was granted cutting rights to a billion feet of lumber in the forests around Westwood (see the description of Westwood which follows).

One of the most delicate and delightful buildings in the town is the tiny Episcopalian Church which, although overshadowed by the huge structures around it, has a peculiar charm all of its own.

A little distance beyond the town, around Mud Creek, are the remains of the devastation which befell the area in August 1924. In that year the Konwakiton glacier melted at a far faster rate than ever recorded and the normally docile mountain streams became rivers of churning mud which destroyed much of the vegetation and left many square miles of landscape under a thick layer of glacial sediment.

Travelling eastwards from McCloud the road passes through dense groves of pines before descending into the pastoral Fall River Valley with its unusual barns set in flat fields of waving wheat.

BARN • FALL RIVER MILLS

Westwood

AN EXPERIMENT IN UTOPIA

Westwood today is a sleepy community in the heart of the timber country. Its huge lumber mills, once the largest in the world are silent and quietly crumbling; the old civic auditorium with its roller-skating rink is boarded up and the days when first-run movies attracted scores of husky lumberjacks to the massive theatre have long since gone.

But the Westwood of the 1920's was a different story. This was a model town, built and run by the Walker family of Minnesota along strict socialistic lines. Wage differentials were minimal, food prices were not inflated, schooling, hospital treatment and communal recreation facilities were provided at nominal cost, sale and consumption of liquor was forbidden, labor agitators were barred and the finest cultural entertainment was provided (Mrs. Walker even gave her own operatic concerts to the apparent delight of the town's "model" citizens). Westwood even boasted a central heating plant which supplied every building and home—the pipes ran under the wooden boardwalks.

Sadly the idealism died. Labor troubles arose and many of the younger men thought the place too straightlaced and left. In 1945 the Walkers sold out and the town began to deteriorate slowly.

OREGON

NEVADA

Redding

downieville■ ■alleghany
nevada city■ Reno

auburn■ ■lotus
Sacramento ■folsom
folsom ■volcano
■mokelumne hill
Stockton

San Francisco ■knights ferry

hornitos■

north

miles 0 20 40 60 80

NORTHERN CALIFORNIA

The Gold Country

The great California Gold Rush is a significant facet of world history. Stories and legends of that period are as familiar in England and Australia as they are in the homes of Mother Lode residents. Without the wealth of romantic folk history which this frantic era produced, one wonders if the Hollywood film studios would ever have gained the prominence they did. The western movie had an enormous impact upon the film-making industry, and even today, with most of the glamor gone from the California studios, European directors continue to churn out the hackneyed themes—in Italian, Spanish and even Bulgarian!

It was the Gold Rush of 1849 which really started the irrepressible growth of California, a growth which has still not peaked. Thousands of pan-wielding pioneers made instant fortunes. Cities arose literally overnight to house and supply the prosperous miners. Land which previously had been considered barren waste, was transformed into rolling wheat fields and pasture. San Francisco and Sacramento became important trading and commerce centers within weeks of the initial gold discovery, although the former experienced occasional problems when most of its able-bodied menfolk joined the rush to the hills.

But it was by no means every miner who found instant wealth in the Mother Lode. The exaggerated optimism of newspapers, editors and journalists around the world did much to create chaos in those narrow Sierra canyons. Tens of thousands of hopeful immigrants attracted by the myths of easy riches, came from as far afield as Australia and New Zealand, only to find despair and bankruptcy after bitter months of fruitless panning in freezing stream beds. One of the individuals to suffer most from the ill fortunes of the minefields was James Wilson Marshall, the man who first discovered gold in California. Marshall was an employee of John Sutter, one of the legendary figures of early California history. While directing the completion of a sawmill at Coloma he found traces of gold in the tailrace. Even though Marshall and Sutter tried hard to claim ownership of the land around Coloma, the rush virtually stampeded them out of the area. Marshall never managed to secure a claim and

spent the last years of his life peddling his auto-
graph to souvenir hunters.

The Mother Lode has many such tales to tell
and the small communities still retain much of
their original character.

Alleghany

THE RIVER OF GOLD

The first settlers in this area were a bunch of
Hawaiian sailors who, in common with hundreds
of prospectors in the early days of the gold rush,
deserted ship at the earliest opportunity and sped
up to the Mother Lode equipped only with mule,
gold pan, pick and blanket.

The Kanaka Creek, named after the Hawai-
ians, proved to be a veritable river of gold. In
fact the ore mined in this area was the highest
grade registered in the mother lode and in the
long mining period which lasted until 1965, an
estimated $50 million of gold was extracted from
the rugged slopes around Alleghany.

Today the town is a small cluster of steep-
roofed buildings which cling precariously to the
hillside. For much of the winter this tiny forgot-
ten settlement is virtually inaccessible.

MAIN STREET
ALLEGHANY

Auburn

PICNICS, HANGINGS AND CIRCUSES

A Frenchman named Claude Chana and three of his countrymen were the first recorded settlers in the Auburn ravine. On May 16, 1848, these fortunate prospectors extracted three large gold nuggets from their very first pan and decided that all omens were in their favor. Within a few weeks a small town settlement with the name of "North Fork Dry Diggins" had sprung up. A year or so later, remnants of the Auburn volunteer regiment of New York found their way into the area and the town became known as Auburn.

At the height of the placer-mining period, it was not unusual for miners around Auburn to make $1,000 a day from small creek claims. One local legend tells of a claim which produced over four cartloads of ore in a day—equivalent to

$16,000! It's small wonder that during the early gold rush, rumors abounded which pictured the Sierras as mountains of solid gold, and were sincerely believed by the great tide of fortune-hunters who flocked to the foothills.

After the placer diggings had extracted most of the surface ores, many towns quietly died. Auburn, however, continued to expand as a major transportation and quartz-mining center. Its fine firehouse, matched only by an even more elaborate version in Nevada City, is evidence of the prosperity which the town experienced during the mining period.

Above the steep-stepped street, which used to be known as Lawyers Row, sits the stately Placer County Courthouse—a remarkably refined structure built in the 1890's. Its site was once used as the public hanging yard, a center of grizzly spectacle during the early rough and tumble days. By all accounts, public hangings were usually festive occasions, often followed by picnics, bull and bear fights or a circus. Unfortunate criminals were invariably dispatched on Sundays in order to attract a good audience—after all the hard working miners deserved occasional diversions!

Downieville

A DUBIOUS REPUTATION

The little community of Downieville sits in a steep alpine setting surrounded by deep, almost inpenetrable forests. It's a quaint town full of churches (note the unusual domed church in the foreground of the sketch) and false front structures which date back to the early days of the Gold Rush.

A little way above the main street is the Relics House—a genuine log cabin which drips with old artifacts of the mining days: bottles, picks, saws and placer pans.

It's had to believe that this idyllic community gained worldwide notoriety as the only town in the gold country to have hanged a woman. She was a Mexican dance hall girl—Juanita—charged with stabbing a miner who, she claimed, continually molested her. It took Downieville a long time to live down the stigma of this execution.

VIEW OVER THE TOWN • DOWNIEVILLE

Folsom

A STORE-KEEPERS PARADISE

During the first few years of the gold boom the area around the town of Folsom contained a number of small mining communities. Negro Bar was founded in 1880 by a group of negro miners on the American River and the nearby town of Mormon Island, which has vanished without a trace, was established by a group of Mormons who had worked for John Sutter at the time of the first gold discovery at Sutters Mill. Samuel

Brannan, the rebellious leader of the California Mormons, set up a prosperous store here and required all miners to tithe one-third of their earnings to the Mormon Church. During 1849-51 most Mormons left to rejoin Brigham Young in Utah but Samuel remained behind, along with much of the tithe money!

In 1856 Captain Joseph Folsom financed the construction of a supply railroad from Sacramento to his newly founded town of Folsom and promoted the town's development as a major marketing center. During the brief but famous interlude of the Pony Express, Folsom became the western terminus of the St. Louis to Sacramento route.

Visitors to the town today are often amazed by the fine group of Victorian mansions which line the steep bluff above the old main street. The Cohn residence which was begun in 1880 (and only completed in 1890) is a perfect example of the stick-and-shingle style. The Burnham House built by a local pharmacist is evidence of the wealth that awaited astute store-keepers in those early days when potatoes could cost $3 a pound, shirts $50, and boots up to $150 a pair!

BURNHAM HOUSE • FOLSOM

Knights Ferry

THE COVERED BRIDGE MYTH

There are many myths surrounding the construction of covered bridges. However, according to responsible authorities they were not built to prevent horses from being panicked by rushing streams; they were not designed as snow guards; nor were they erected expressly for the use of starry-eyed lovers as some of the more romantic of California's historians would seem to believe. In fact the covered bridge was a pragmatic solution to the problem of continuous maintenance which plagued the old plank bridge.

There are only a handful of such structures remaining in California, the most well known being in the De Laveaga Park in Santa Cruz. The bridge at Knights Ferry, built in 1862, is still standing which would seem to support the claim for the design's durability. Prior to the bridging of the Stanislaus River, William Knight operated a ferry during the initial months of the gold rush and records show that he regularly made a clear $500 a day from the thousands of would-be miners who poured into the Mother Lode. Unfortunately, Mr. Knight was killed in a shootout in 1849 and was unable to enjoy his riches!

CHURCH • HORNITOS

Hornitos

THE HAUNT OF JOAQUIN MURIETA

Hornitos was founded by a gang of Mexicans who had been kicked out of the nearby town of Quartzburg. In later years it became a favorite haunt of the bandit, Murieta, who is credited with having provided himself with special underground escape routes for times when things got a little too hot.

Thanks to the capricious writings of John Rollin Ridge, fact and fiction merge into a romantic blur when Murieta, the "Robin Hood of the Southern Mines" is discussed. Ridge wrote his famous "Life and Adventures of Joaquin Murieta" in 1854 to cater to readers anxious to idealize the larger-than-life men who populated the early mining camps.

Today the town is a peaceful community with its little church set in the fields above the main square. Around the church can be found these strange raised burial mounds which the Mexicans

called "hornitos" or "little ovens." Apparently the rocky ground was just too hard in which to dig graves, so the practical residents merely laid the coffin on the grass and built a rock casing around it.

Lotus

THE STRANGE TOWN NAMES OF
THE MOTHER LODE

The old, tree-shaded cemeteries of the gold country are some of the most fascinating in California. They are silent records of lives spent in arduous toil; of the days when medicine was scarce and parents considered themselves fortunate if half their offspring reached maturity. This tiny cemetery on a little hill behind the sleepy town of Lotus has many such tales to tell.

Lotus was never a very significant town in the Mother Lode and today is notable only for its charming red schoolhouse, built in 1869, which was once an art gallery and is now a private residence.

There was a tendency among the early miners to bestow upon their communities, descriptive and explanatory names. Lotus was fortunate to retain its unusual but romantic title but towns like Rough 'n Ready, Pokerville, Fiddletown, Chinese Camp, Rawhide, Dutch Flat, and Yankee Jims are destined to retain their strange-sounding names in perpetuity. Fortunately for the communities involved, even more explicit titles, such as Down and Out, No-Good, Wildcat, Hangtown, Growlersburg, and Sweet Vengeance, have long since been abandoned in favor of more respectful names. Growlersburg is now Georgetown, Hangtown is Placerville, and Sweet Vengeance is Browns Valley.

A few miles to the east of Lotus is Coloma, the home of John Sutter's sawmill and the birthplace of the gold rush. As with many of the early towns, Coloma had a short life. By 1852, only three years after the initial rush, most of its 10,000 inhabitants had left for other parts of the Mother Lode in search of elusive bonanzas.

OLD SCHOOL HOUSE • LOTUS

Mokelumne Hill

HOME OF E CLAMPUS VITUS

Mokelumne Hill is one of the most delightful of the gold country towns. The Hotel Leger, with its tastefully restored bar is typical of the larger hotels which once flourished in abundance throughout the Mother Lode. Down the hill, where the narrow main street curves out of the town, stands the tall austere Oddfellows Hall, constructed of light brown "rhyolite tuff"—a material used in many of the mining towns' more prominent buildings.

Fraternal lodges played a major role in the early mining days, providing otherwise disorganized communities with a civic and cultural backbone. The most respected fraternities were, of course, the Masons and Oddfellows although J. H. Zumwalt, a resident of Mokelumne Hill, grew impatient with the snobbishness and secrecy of these organizations, and founded his own non-fraternity known as E. Clampus Vitus in 1850. This

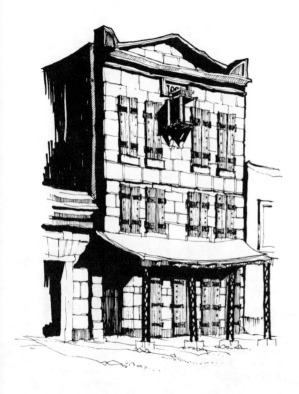

ODDFELLOWS HALL • MOKELUMNE HILL

HOTEL LEGER · MOKELUMNE HILL

OLD MINE · JACKSON

body of disrespectful souls was presided over by the Noble Grand Humbug and members were sworn to a life of absolute enjoyment, joviality and self-indulgence.

According to local records, life in Mokelumne Hill was not all fun and games. During one particularly hectic period, more than seventeen murders were recorded in the same number of weeks. In addition, claim wars were common, the most notable of which were the Chilean and French Wars. In the latter instance, a group of French miners raised the French flag above their prosperous diggings on a hill overlooking the town. Irate citizens booted them out of the area and, in righteous indignation, took over their claims.

A few miles to the south of Mokelumne Hill are the remains of the Kennedy Mine which was founded in 1856 and boasted some of the longest shafts in the world—over 5000 feet deep. The mine, which operated until 1942, is still largely intact and the huge tailing wheels constructed in 1912 contrast sharply with the early equipment such as this gold wash machine used by the early placer miners.

Nevada City

CUZIN' JACKS AND CORNISH PASTIES

One of the largest and best preserved of the Mother Lode towns, Nevada City, was the city of "cuzin Jacks"—a somewhat disrespectful term which described the Cornish tin miners whose one ambition, after reaching California, was to amass sufficient capital to bring over the rest of the family—aunts, uncles, cousins, and nephews. It was the expertise of these miners, however, which made Nevada City and nearby Grass Valley, two of the most prosperous communities in the gold country. The only obvious sign today of the once powerful Cornish influence are the "Cornish pasties," a sort of meat and vegetable mash wrapped in crisp baked pastry. These delicious morsels are for sale in bars and restaurants throughout the area.

Nevada City's development is a familiar story, typical of most mining communities. Its early names included Deer Creek Dry Diggins, Coyoteville, and Caldwell's Upper Store. It began as a tent town and slowly became a haphazard collection of clapboard shacks which were constantly being razed by fire. A particularly disastrous conflagration in 1856 led to the establishment of some of the most efficient and well equipped firefighting teams in the Mother Lode. In all, three separate fire houses were constructed, all of which exist today.

FIREHOUSE GROUP • NEVADA CITY

Remnants of the gold mining era abound. The first hydraulic mining, a process which literally washed away hillsides to release gold ores, was practiced on nearby American Hill in 1882. In Grass Valley is the huge Pelton Wheel—a supereffective waterwheel which was installed in 1896 at the North Star Mining Company and operated continuously for more than forty years. The efficiency of this design is such that similar wheels are still being manufactured in the East.

The National Hotel and the fine Victorian mansions which abound in Nevada City, all tell of an era of immense wealth and prosperity. According to local stories, this section of the Mother Lode was so rich in gold that miners were continually digging up nuggets in the town's main street, until gun-toting irate merchants, who foresaw the possible elimination of their stores by overenthusiastic miners put a stop to the activity. Nevada City's steep main street could be a Hollywood film set. Hardly a building is out of place; even the streetlamps have recently been changed to Colonial-style gas lamps and the magnificently ornate firehouse, just off the main street, is maintained in white Victorian splendor as a museum.

VICTORIAN MANSION
NEVADA CITY

Volcano

CULTURE IN THE MOTHER-LODE

The small town of Volcano nestles in a little wooded hollow, surrounded on three sides by steep mountains which, the original prospectors thought, resembled volcanoes—hence the name.

Volcano's citizens, who consisted initially of the remnants of the New York 8th Regiment Mexican war volunteers, were a civic-minded bunch, and aware of the cultural needs of the rapidly growing population. In addition to the 30-odd saloons and three breweries, the town boasted the first debating society, library and observatory in California.

The proud citizens were also anxious to protect their culture-prone town from a planned take over by Confederates during the Civil War. One showing of the town's cannon, "Old Abe", soon put an end to that problem. The cannon is on display in a small building at the top end of town.

MAIN STREET • VOLCANO

The Coast

The coastal region consists of two distinct sections. The area south of San Francisco around the Monterey peninsula is often referred to as the "cradle of California" (much to the annoyance of citizens of San Diego!). It was from here that Father Junipero Serra directed his program of Mission building and Indian conversion, which was to provide the first thin line of "civilization" in California, along the "Camino Real." The towns of Monterey and San Juan Bautista are rich in the relics of this important period.

The coastline north of San Francisco, by contrast, remained virtually undisturbed until the latter half of the nineteenth century. Prior to that time the only residents along the wild seashore were half-starved bands of Indians and a group of hardy Russian fur-hunters based at Fort Ross.

The impetus for coastal development came mainly as a result of San Francisco's rapid growth both during and after the gold rush. This had been on such a scale that any form of rationally planned expansion was impossible—as a result clapboard buildings crowded together on every available piece of land and fires extracted a regular toll of death and destruction. Between 1849 and 1857, the city was almost totally burnt down six times! Thus it became necessary to ensure a regular supply of lumber from the Redwood forests along the northern coast to enable rapid reconstruction following each holocaust. As inland roads were virtually nonexistent the lumber had to be hauled to San Franciso by boat. Virtually every small cove (or "dog-hole") offered potentials as a loading point. Communities such as Mendocino, Eureka and Noyo developed as lumbering centers. The latter was founded by the famous lumber-baron, C. H. Johnson whose ingenuity produced the unique "Skunk Railroad" which provided the first land link between the coast and the interior.

As the economic supply of Redwood dwindled, many of the coastal towns became important fishing ports. Inland communities such as Boonville, Bodega and Ferndale also grew as agricultural centers, populated largely by Danish, Swiss and Portuguese farmers.

Today the coastal region seems little changed from almost a century ago; its small towns are some of the most attractive in California.

OLD SCHOOL · BODEGA

Bodega

A RUSSIAN OUTPOST

Bodega was once a Russian settlement bearing the name "Kuskoff." Founded by Ivan Alexander Kuskoff in 1881 it was one of a series of bases on the American continent for the Russian-American Fur Company. The company's exploits on the California Coast were curtailed in 1841 when the American Government made it clear that the Czar's ambitions to annex the coastal region were likely to meet with fierce resistance. So the Russians left and the town became the center of a flourishing agriculture and forestry area.

Today Bodega is a small pastoral community boasting a fine schoolhouse and a New England styled church, St. Teresa's, built in 1862. The town's only recent claim to fame is that it provided some of the locational shots for Hitchcock's film "The Birds," in 1962.

Boonville

THE BOONTLINGS OF BOONT

The residents of this quiet pastoral community amuse themselves and visitors by communicating in a strange gobbledeguck, known locally as Boontling.

A sign in the town's cafe reads:

*"Our gorms are ball, our zeese is hot;
some regions de-hiig you, but we will
not."*

To the laymen, it's nonsense but to the Boontlingers of Boonville it's a perfectly normal statement in Boont-language. The translation reads:

*Our food is good, our coffee hot; some
places cheat you, but we will not."*

This strange language (no one seems too clear why it was invented or how it stuck) contains bits of Swedish, Italian and German as well as disguised references to local individuals. For example, the word "zeese" (coffee) stems from the unfortunate Z. C. Blevens, a one-time resident notorious for his lousy coffee.

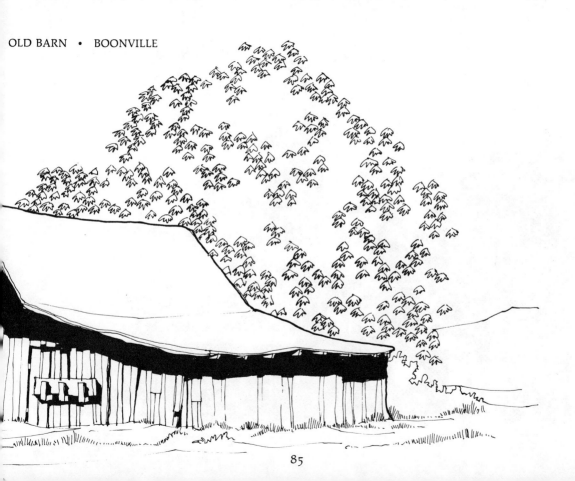

Eureka

MONUMENT TO A LUMBER BARON

The Carson mansion, which sits in all its Gothic fantasy on a prominent knoll overlooking the historic quarter of town, is said to be the most photographed building in the U.S.A. It was the brainchild of the Lumber Baron, William Carson, who came to California in 1850 to dredge for gold on the Trinity River. Carson soon recognized the need for lumber particularly in San Francisco and in partnership with John Dolbeer (inventor of the side-spool donkey engine) made a huge fortune, felling the gigantic Redwoods of the Humboldt Forest.

Carson decided he needed a house appropriate to his financial status and instructed his architects to design an edifice which would stand as an example to the world of the infinite glories of wood as a building material. It took an army of 150 carpenters to complete the task.

Across from the mansion is a smaller and more restrained Victorian home in which Carson lived during the construction of his monument and which he later gave to his son.

The early settlers in Eureka were an unruly lot with an apparent intense dislike of all non Anglo-Saxon residents in the area. On February 25, 1860 a group of them rowed out to Indian Island, one of the several such islands in Arcata Bay, and massacred all the Indian families camped there. It turned out that many of the warriors of the small tribe were away hunting during the massacre but upon their return, they began months of bitter skirmishes with the white settlers. Angry residents of Eureka who opposed the outrage, including the famous Bret Harte, were advised to leave town or meet a fate similar to that of the Indians.

A second incident is equally indicative of the formidable character of early north coast settlers. In 1885 anti-Chinese prejudice had reached a peak in the town and on February 6 all residents of Chinatown were given 24 hours to leave town. Within a few days all the orientals in the county had been forced out and their property confiscated. Even today there are almost no orientals living in Humboldt and Chinese crews on ships visiting Eureka still refuse to go ashore.

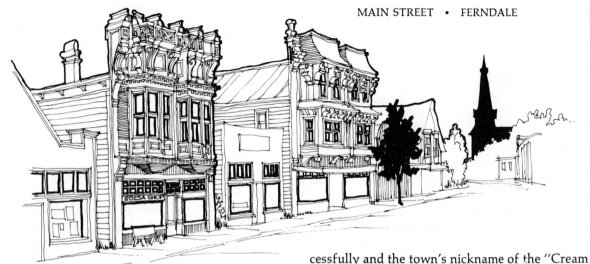

Ferndale

AN UNSPOILED COMMUNITY

This delightful Victorian village, located a few miles west of 101, south of Eureka, was founded in 1852 by a farmer, Seth Louis Shaw, who was later joined by groups of Danish, Portuguese and Italian pioneers. It is one of the few locations in California where herds of Jersey cattle thrive suc-cessfully and the town's nickname of the "Cream City" is well deserved.

Ferndale is rich in Victorian architecture; some of the finest examples of "carpenter Gothic" styles in Northern California, can be found along its quiet streets. Other of the town's major build-ings such as the Portuguese Hall, tell of the area's rich ethnic background.

Progress in the shape of brash commercial de-velopment and dismal housing tracts seems to have passed the town by. It's a perfect unspoiled enclave of yesteryear.

TYPICAL VICTORIAN HOUSE • FERNDALE

MENDOCINO STREET SCENE

Mendocino

A FORTUNATE RENAISSANCE

The New England styled town of Mendocino is perched daintily on a rugged rocky promontory at the mouth of the Big River. It was known originally as Meiggsville, after the San Francisco politician and speculator Harry Meiggs who developed the area as a lumbering center until 1854, when he fled the country pursued by angry creditors. His mill at Big River declined until it was finally sold to the famous C. R. Johnson and his Union Lumber Company at Fort Bragg.

Johnson operated in the area until 1937 and then abandoned the town which subsequently entered a period of stagnation. In the 50's Mendocino experienced a renaissance as an artists' colony and since that time it has developed all the good and bad qualities of a tourist town. Nevertheless it still remains one of the most attractive of the coastal communities.

Monterey

THE CRADLE OF CALIFORNIA

Monterey is perhaps the most written-about town in California, which is perhaps understandable as this wild stretch of coastline was virtually the birthplace of California. Almost every legendary figure who appears in the annals of early California history either lived, visited or was chased out of this small seashore community.

Although Monterey Bay was "discovered" as early as 1542 by Juan Rodriguez Cabrillo and later visited by Sebastian Vizcaino in 1602, it was not until that sturdy little Majorcan priest, Father Junipero Serra arrived in 1770 that the area was finally settled. Father Serra was born Miguel José Serra in Majorca in 1713 and after teaching philosophy in Spain for fifteen years was sent to Mexico City to help in Spanish efforts to convert local Indians. His outstanding popularity with the primitive tribes made him a suitable candidate for the Alta California missionary expedition, headed by Gaspar de Portola.

After founding California's first mission in San Diego in 1769 he joined a second expedition which reached Monterey Bay and there founded the Mission San Carlos Borromeo Del Rio Carmelo. This handsome structure became his headquarters from which he developed the chain of missions from San Diego to Sonoma.

Until the Gold Rush of 1848-49 Monterey remained the capital of Alta California and its many remaining historic buildings are silent record of the one-time importance of this small town. The pantiled Customs house which overlooks Fisherman's Wharf is the oldest government building on the Pacific coast and continued to collect revenues from foreign trading ships until 1846. A little distance away is California's first theater built in 1846, which in addition to its primary

DOC RICKETT'S LAB • MONTEREY

entertainment function also served as a sailor's boarding house and a home for the sturdy crews of the old whaling ships.

A notable feature of the town's early adobe architecture is its two-story construction complete with balconies. This is a particularly unusual refinement with such an unwieldy material as adobe and it has been suggested that the "Monterey style" as it is called, was the creation of some of the early New England sailors who regularly visited the port town.

Cannery Row, located a mile or so away from the historical area, formed the scenario for John Steinbeck's famous novel and is indicative of Monterey's post-capital role as a fishing community. Most of the large corrugated structures have long been abandoned due to the disappearance of the sardines in the late 1940's but the area still remains one of Monterey's most popular tourist stops. Considerable pressure is evident to turn the area into another commercial strip dominated by parking lots and souvenir stalls. There's even talk that Doc Rickett's laboratory might have to go! Readers familiar with Steinbeck's "Cannery Row" will be amused by the irony of such a idea.

CANNERY ROW
MONTEREY

Moss Landing

Moss Landing with its rambling flea market, crowded harbor and antique stores, is a jumbled little community located a few miles north of Monterey. Legend has it that, during the town's boom days as a port, supply wagons from the Salinas Valley farms would line up for five miles waiting to unload their produce. Although such stories may be somewhat exaggerated, Moss Landing was once a prominent center of the whaling industry and during the peak of the whaling season (February-October), five of those blubber-laden mammals would be processed weekly. Somehow the unfortunate residents managed to put up with the sickly odors which such an industry inevitably generated until the early 1920's when the Board of Health declared the plant a public menace. However, the situation was hardly improved when a fish reduction plant took its place!

ANTIQUES ROW • MOSS LANDING

Noyo

C. R. JOHNSON & "THE SKUNK"

Noyo and the adjoining town of Fort Bragg owe their initial fortunes to Charles R. Johnson, the lumber tycoon who, after much effort, convinced the tight-fisted and skeptical investors of the East that the giant Redwood forests of the California coast really did exist. Johnson founded the Union Lumber Company in 1891. Then he hacked and switchbacked his famous "Skunk" railroad over the coastal range linking Fort Bragg and Noyo to Willits on the Russian River and thus opened a much needed and direct link to San Francisco.

In addition, this ambitious lumberman hired an army of Chinese laborers to carry the railroad almost 1150 feet through a ridge which separated the Noyo River from the adjoining forest in the Pudding Creek Valley—a spectacular achievement at that time.

As the lumber industry went into decline around the turn of the century, Noyo turned to fishing as its prime economy and today is one of the most popular centers for sport fishing on the northern coast.

San Juan Bautista

A TUMULTUOUS TOWN

It's hard to imagine that this delightfully historical community with its fine Mission Plaza and "old-west" main street was the focal point of much of California's tumultuous early history.

Until José Tiburcio Castro was appointed Civil Administrator (following the mission secularization decree in 1835) the Mission had existed quietly since its founding in 1797 and had been particularly successful in converting local Indians (4,300 Indians are buried in the old cemetery). Tiburcio twice used the town as a rallying point against Mexican Governors of California and then turned on Captain John Fremont who was over-extending his "surveying" expedition in California. Fremont in turn used the town in 1846 to assemble his "California Battalion" and the bandit, Tiburcio Vasquez, adopted San Juan as a base for his notorious exploits. The jail must have been one of the town's most valuable assets.

Sanity, however, existed in the form of Angelo Zanetta, a famed restaurateur from New Orleans, whose French dishes, served at his Plaza Hotel, were renowned throughout the region.

MISSION PLAZA • SAN JUAN BAUTISTA

WINEMA THEATRE • SCOTIA

Scotia

ONE OF THE LAST COMPANY TOWNS

In the densely wooded valley of the Eel River, a few miles south of the Port of Eureka, is situated one of the last remaining all-company towns in the U.S.A. Owned by the Pacific Lumber Company, Scotia is a sturdy little community boasting one of the most elaborately detailed theaters in California, built entirely out of roughly finished Redwood.

The company has been in continuous operation since 1869 and numerous fires, floods and the occasional earthquakes have provided only temporary setbacks to its lumber operation. Old photographs in the Company Museum, located in another magnificent wooden structure, tell of the days of gargantuan lumberjacks, huge cookhouse dinners, 20-ox teams which used to drag the lumber from the slopes to the plant, and the powerful little steam engines which zig-zagged their way around the coastal mountain ranges.

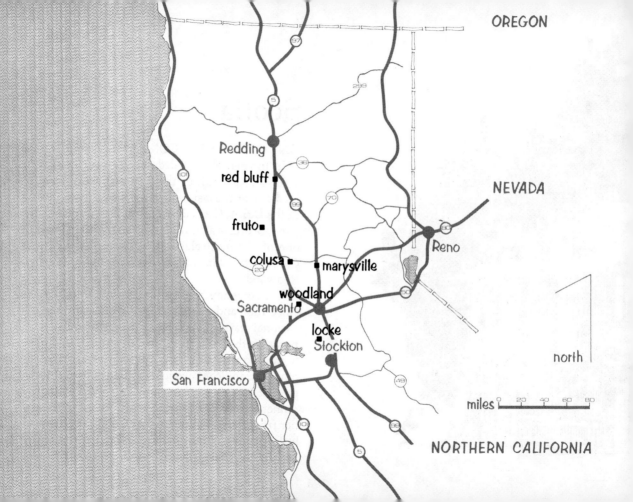

The Sacramento Valley

Jedediah Smith, the famous explorer of early California, visited the Valley in 1828 and wrote:

"It is an area where the creator has scattered a more than ordinary share of his bounties."

A few years later John Sutter, a man of German-Swiss origin, who had fled his homeland due to the pressure of his ailing financial affairs, arrived in the valley and persuaded the Mexican Government to provide him with a generous land grant. In return Sutter undertook to safeguard the area from "adventurers and scoundrels," by which the Mexicans referred particularly to American bounty-hunters masquerading under the title of "surveyors."

Sutter took his status very seriously. He even formed his own kingdom known as New Helvetia and constructed his fort on the site of what later became the city of Sacramento. He embarked upon a whole series of wild profit-making schemes which were as financially disastrous as they were imaginative. Even his son, who joined his father immediately prior to the gold rush, finally gave up all hope of making his father a businessman and left for Mexico in despair. Nevertheless, for all his failures, John Sutter remains one of California's most fascinating folk-heroes.

The rapid development of the Sacramento Valley was primarily a result of the 1849 gold rush. The unprecedented influx of settlers generated a need for massive food supplies and an efficient network of distribution centers. Towns such as Marysville and Red Bluff grew up rapidly as a result of heavy traffic on the Sacramento River. Woodland and Colusa were both examples of prosperous farming centers; the former boasted that during the 1860's it contained more millionaires relative to the population size than any other city in the world.

During the early years, the valley suffered continuously from disastrous floods, the "raised" houses in Marysville are indicative of this regular phenomenon. It was not until the Chinese laborers returned to the valley from the Mother Lode that comprehensive levee building was undertaken. Locke, on the delta, is one of the few remaining examples of the valley's once prolific Chinese communities.

Colusa

THE VIRTUOUS LYNCHERS

This neat little town which clings to a bend in the Sacramento River was founded as the center of navigation in 1850. Unfortunately, it soon lost this status to Tehema which subsequently gave way to Red Bluff. However, the town managed to retain its title of County Seat of Colusa County and is today the center of one of the richest rice-growing areas in the U.S.A.

Colusa's relatively respectful history is marred only by one incident. It appears that during the anti-Chinese era of the 1880's, a local lynch mob hanged a young Chinese servant for supposedly murdering the wife of a prominent rancher. Ironically the coroner's report praised the lynchers and condemned the jurymen who had sentenced the unfortunate Chinaman to mere life imprisonment!

The downtown area contains a number of interesting buildings, including this elaborate Oddfellows Hall constructed in 1889. Outside the town, in the flat valley fields, fascinating remnants of the old farming days can be found. This steam-powered tractor is a fine specimen.

Fruto

RESTING PLACE OF THE NYE FAMILY

The area of low rolling hills around Fruto is one of the most delightfully pastoral regions in the Sacramento Valley, rich in wild life and spotted with little pieces of romantic dilapidation such as this once fine house on the edge of the village.

As its name would suggest, Fruto was once famous for its orchards, many of which were tended by Chinese laborers who had moved away from the Sierra foothills after the gold rush had dwindled.

The lonely cemetery perched on a bleak hilltop contains most of the ill-fated Nye family whose members were wiped out by a fierce flu epidemic in 1918.

Locke

A CHINESE COMMUNITY ON THE DELTA

The Delta with its flat horizons, its little creeks and reed-edged lakes is one of the most unusual and captivating landscapes in California. Its towns: Rio Vista, Clarksburg, Walnut Grove, and Locke, all crouch along the banks of the Sacramento River as if nervously awaiting the next flood.

Floods of course were a common feature in this area during the early days, and it was not until the latter years of the gold rush era that concerted efforts were made to control the winter moods of the Sacramento River by the construction of massive levees. As with so many of California's early development projects, it was the Chinese who provided the bulk of the labor—at virtually slave rates!

Locke, one of the most unusual of the Delta communities, is named after Miss Alice Locke who leased the land to a number of Chinese families in the early 1900's. The town subsequently grew up on two levels, the top half of the buildings face onto the main levee road, the bottom

THEATRE STAIRCASE • LOCKE

half onto a sunken main street which forms the heart of this unique town. Narrow staircases such as the one shown in the sketch provide a quick link between the two levels.

Locke once had a notorious reputation as a gambling, opium and prostitution town, but today it is a model of docility and calm. The main street is almost unbearably quiet on hot delta afternoons. Of course there are occasional outbursts which normally center around Al's (the Wop's) Bar and Restaurant. This amazing place with its antique-strewn bar is known throughout the Delta for its huge steak and peanut butter and jelly sandwich lunches.

Walnut Grove, located a mile or so south of Locke, is a slightly larger community but contains many of Locke's unusual architectural features including a dual-level main street.

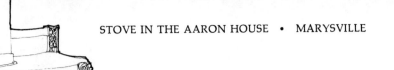

Marysville

A TOWN OF HARDY SOCIALITES

Many towns in the Sacramento Valley owe their past prosperity to the early days of the gold rush when the thousands of bearded, bedraggled prospectors in the Sierras paid miniature fortunes for basic agricultural produce. In those days prices such as $1 for an egg, $3 for a pound of potatoes and $6 for a few slices of salt pork were often considered the norm.

Marysville, located at the confluence of the Yuba and Feather Rivers, was one such town that prospered during those pioneering days. It was founded in 1850 by Charles Covillaud who named it after his wife Mary Murphy, one of the few survivors from the disastrous Donner Party.

For all its wealth and importance as a major marketing center and head of navigation of the Feather River, Marysville's development was not without its problems. During the early 1850's the legendary bandit Joaquin Murietta terrorized the region around the town. Also, until the early 1900's Marysville was plagued with terrible floods although, according to local sources, this rarely affected the social life of the town. During one particularly bad period in 1853 the resplendent Merchants Hotel was totally flooded out at ground level at the time of the New Year's Eve "Grand Ball." Not to be outdone, the hardy socialites rented boats and rowed their way to the second floor ballroom.

The impact of floods upon the town can be seen in the architecture. Most of the older homes have ground floors at second floor level, linked to the sidewalk by ornate sets of steps. Many of the homes are also indicative of the wealth which the town once enjoyed. The miniature castle, owned by the Aaron family, is particularly notable and today this unusual building contains an interesting museum of victorian artifacts including a splendidly ornate kitchen stove.

115

Red Bluff

A "HARD PLACE"

The town of Red Bluff is extremely proud of its collection of Victorian mansions which occupy what was once the exclusive sector of the town west of the main street. Although many of the mansions today are in desperate need of renovation, the Kelly Briggs House (now a museum) is a fine example of Italianate design. The clock tower on the Cone-Kimball building was built in 1886 and with its seven roaring lion gargoyles is the town's most prominent landmark.

From 1850-70 Red Bluff enjoyed enormous prosperity as the head of navigation on the Sacramento River, serving much of northern California and southern Oregon. During that brief era the town developed a notorious reputation as a "hard place," replete with gamblers, horse thieves and gay girls. Today, however, Red Bluff has gone the way of most tumultuous towns and has adopted a mantle of calm and respectability.

Woodland

THE BEST BEER IN CALIFORNIA

To the casual motorist, Woodland would appear to be just another California town with a slightly wilted main street. Not so! Take a look up the streets on the south side of Main Street and you'll find one of the finest collections of mid-Victorian architecture in the Sacramento Valley. Almost every style and influence is evident—in some instances all gloriously displayed in a single building.

The Gable mansion, although sadly dilapidated, is one of the most elaborate mansions in the area, and the detailing on the windows and porticoes of other homes is immaculate.

Woodland once contained scores of "overnight" millionaires, who made their vast fortunes supplying the Sierra gold towns with locally grown produce. Many of the inhabitants were of German extraction, and the town was renowned for the superb quality of its beer. It was produced from local barley, which was of such a high standard that much of it was exported to the world-famous breweries of Bavaria.

PORTICO DETAIL • WOODLAND

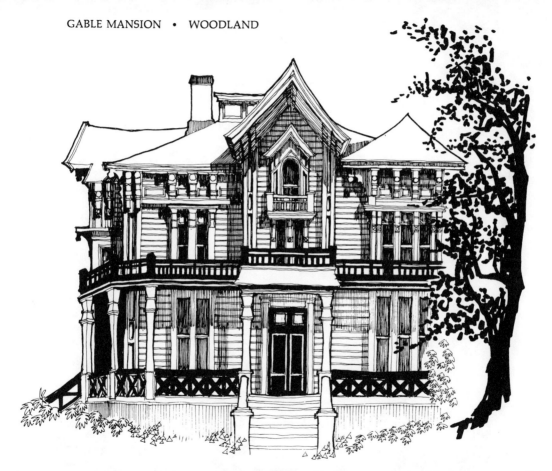

INDEX

NOTES

NOTES

NOTES

$1.95 EACH—WESTERN TRAVEL & LEISURE GUIDEBOOKS FROM THE WARD RITCHIE PRESS

Trips for the Day, Weekend or Longer

MOST BOOKS HAVE PHOTOGRAPHS AND MAPS.

QUANTITY		TOTAL
☐	**BACKYARD TREASURE HUNTING**	$
☐	**BAJA CALIFORNIA:** Vanished Missions, Lost Treasures, Strange Stories True and Tall	$
☐	**BICYCLE TOURING IN LOS ANGELES**	$
☐	**EAT,** A Toothsome Tour of L.A.'s Specialty Restaurants	$
☐	**EXPLORING BIG SUR, MONTEREY AND CARMEL**	$
☐	**EXPLORING CALIFORNIA BYWAYS, No. 2,** In and Around Los Angeles	$
☐	**EXPLORING CALIFORNIA BYWAYS, No. 3,** Desert Country	$
☐	**EXPLORING CALIFORNIA BYWAYS, No. 4,** Mountain Country	$
☐	**EXPLORING CALIFORNIA BYWAYS, No. 5,** Historic Sites of California	$
☐	**EXPLORING CALIFORNIA BYWAYS, No. 6,** Owens Valley	$
☐	**EXPLORING CALIFORNIA BYWAYS, No. 7,** An Historical Sketchbook	$
☐	**EXPLORING CALIFORNIA FOLKLORE**	$
☐	**EXPLORING THE GHOST TOWN DESERT**	$
☐	**EXPLORING HISTORIC CALIFORNIA**	$
☐	**EXPLORING THE MOTHER LODE COUNTRY**	$
☐	**EXPLORING SMALL TOWNS, No. 1**—Southern California	$
☐	**EXPLORING SMALL TOWNS, No. 2**—Northern California	$
☐	**EXPLORING THE UNSPOILED WEST, Vol. 1**	$
☐	**EXPLORING THE UNSPOILED WEST, Vol. 2**	$
☐	**FEET FIRST:** Walks through Ten Los Angeles Areas	$
☐	**GREAT BIKE TOURS IN NORTHERN CALIFORNIA**	$
☐	**GUIDEBOOK TO THE CANYONLANDS COUNTRY**	$
☐	**GUIDEBOOK TO THE COLORADO DESERT OF CALIFORNIA**	$
☐	**GUIDEBOOK TO THE FEATHER RIVER COUNTRY**	$
☐	**GUIDEBOOK TO THE LAKE TAHOE COUNTRY, Vol. I.** Echo Summit, Squaw Valley and the California Shore	$
☐	**GUIDEBOOK TO THE LAKE TAHOE COUNTRY, Vol. II.** Alpine County, Donner-Truckee, and the Nevada Shore	$

[MORE BOOKS AND ORDER FORM ON OTHER SIDE]

- ☐ GUIDEBOOK TO LAS VEGAS — $ _____
- ☐ GUIDEBOOK TO LOST WESTERN TREASURE — $ _____
- ☐ GUIDEBOOK TO THE MISSIONS OF CALIFORNIA — $ _____
- ☐ GUIDEBOOK TO THE MOUNTAINS OF SAN DIEGO AND ORANGE COUNTIES — $ _____
- ☐ GUIDEBOOK TO THE NORTHERN CALIFORNIA COAST, VOL. I, Highway 1 — $ _____
- ☐ GUIDEBOOK TO PUGET SOUND — $ _____
- ☐ GUIDEBOOK TO RURAL CALIFORNIA — $ _____
- ☐ GUIDEBOOK TO THE SACRAMENTO DELTA COUNTRY — $ _____
- ☐ GUIDEBOOK TO THE SAN BERNARDINO MOUNTAINS OF CALIFORNIA, Including Lake Arrowhead and Big Bear — $ _____
- ☐ GUIDEBOOK TO THE SAN GABRIEL MOUNTAINS OF CALIFORNIA — $ _____
- ☐ GUIDEBOOK TO SALTWATER FISHING IN SOUTHERN CALIFORNIA — $ _____
- ☐ GUIDEBOOK TO THE SPAS OF NORTHERN CALIFORNIA — $ _____
- ☐ GUIDEBOOK TO VANCOUVER ISLAND — $ _____
- ☐ HIKING THE SANTA BARBARA BACKCOUNTRY — $ _____
- ☐ SABRETOOTH CATS AND IMPERIAL MAMMOTHS — $ _____
- ☐ SKI LOS ANGELES — $ _____
- ☐ WHERE TO TAKE YOUR CHILDREN IN NEVADA — $ _____
- ☐ WHERE TO TAKE YOUR CHILDREN IN NORTHERN CALIFORNIA — $ _____
- ☐ WHERE TO TAKE YOUR CHILDREN IN SOUTHERN CALIFORNIA — $ _____
- ☐ WHERE TO TAKE YOUR GUESTS IN SOUTHERN CALIFORNIA — $ _____
- ☐ YOUR LEISURE TIME . . . HOW TO ENJOY IT — $ _____

THE WARD RITCHIE PRESS
474 S. Arroyo Parkway, Pasadena, Calif. 91105

Please send me the Western Travel and Leisure Guidebooks I have checked.
I am enclosing $ _____ (check or money order). Please include 25¢
per copy to cover mailing costs. California residents add state sales tax.

Name _____

Address _____

City _____ State _____ Zip Code _____